T0356128

Pause the Document

Pause the Document

Mónica de la Torre

NIGHTBOAT BOOKS
NEW YORK

ISBN: 978-1-643-62246-0

DESIGN AND TYPESETTING BY KIT SCHLUTER
TYPESET IN ADOBE TEXT PRO & BIG CASLON

CATALOGING-IN-PUBLICATION DATA IS AVAILABLE
FROM THE LIBRARY OF CONGRESS

NIGHTBOAT BOOKS
NEW YORK
WWW.NIGHTBOAT.ORG

TABLE OF CONTENTS

＊

FELIZA

Greedy for blossoms, euphoria
at the wind's snapping a branch
for me to redeem. I let Shadow
trample the buds.

Later, when I wound the pit
of an avocado, it bleeds
before my eyes.

Between ages we run
out of eggs, chrono-
biology's downside. My still lifes.

Play mad, she instructs: *¡Hágase la loca!*

Push the language through the hourglass.

PARABLE

trees, pillars in nature's temple, speaking
vague, perplexing words, "shimmers of verbal nuance"
often nonsense in this language, obfuscation
confuses paroles easily becomes *palabras confusas*
not to be taken for "confused" or "subdued words"
the adjective describes the words' effect on their recipient, not
their own state—the syntax of placement is key
do they utter "darkling whispers"
is theirs "a soft language, half strange, half understood"

       their messages ramifying

*

    AVISO: LA PALABRA *PALABRA* NO ESTÁ EN EL DICCIONARIO
      (Diccionario histórico de la lengua española)

palabra, metathesis of the Latin *parabola*, from the Greek *parabolē*, a
comparison, a juxtaposition: *para-* "alongside" and *bolē*

          "a throwing, casting, beam, ray"

parable, doublet of *parole*

comparison becomes narration in vulgar Latin and *parabola* becomes *palabra*

   , the word for *word*

   Math.: A *parabola* is a curve where any point is equidistant from a
   fixed point (the focus) and a fixed straight line (the directrix)

an instructive allegory: if an utterance is a curve, all of its points are at an equal but growing distance from its focus

a line of verse is not to be taken for a directrix

*

confused, doublet of *confound*

confusioun c. 1300 "overthrow, ruin" from Old French "disorder, confusion, shame" (11c.)

confound, c. 1300, "to condemn, curse," also "to destroy utterly"; from Anglo-French *confoundre*, Old French *confondre* (12c.)

"crush, ruin, disgrace"

all from the Latin *confundere*: *com* "together" and *fundere* "to pour"

"to confuse, jumble together, bring into disorder" especially of the mind or senses, "disconcert, perplex"

SIN ORDEN NI CONCIERTO

*

Old English *word* "speech, talk, utterance, sentence, statement, news, report, word,"

from Proto-Indo-European *were-* "speak, say."

*

A girl stands alone on the road. Her thoughts are in a language other than this one. She takes in a playground abutting a gully outside a housing complex at the southern edge of the city: an empty swing set on a concrete platform. Stray dogs on the other side of the wire fence. Wind gusts rustle the foliage of surrounding trees. They speak to her for the first time, yet she can't put what they say into any of the words she knows. She contemplates the dance that initiates the drift of spores allowing the trees to go on multiplying.

SAUCER MAGNOLIA

Let the writing follow the trees, was the instruction,
so I went on a walk and later in circles
to get better views of specimens most often standing
for variability and many-sidedness.
I gravitated toward this one, swayed
by its unmistakable tepals—petals
identical to sepals except for the carousel effect
of their terms' transposed consonants.
Its cup-sized blooms captivated me,
much like the beetles bumbling their way
into them and getting trapped overnight,
by design, to ensure cross-pollination.

This ornamental with ample name recognition
 "as common as fertilizer at every garden
center," is "precocious" and "reliable year in
and year out." First among flowering trees,
it flaunts its fleshy blossoms earlier than most:

> "[it] can look stunning one bright late winter or early spring afternoon and with
> an overnight temperature drop to 25 or 28 degrees become a mass of limp brown
> tepals the next day."

Only a fool would disagree it's a billboard for spring:
fragile, downy buds—survivors of the season's
swings—showing themselves triumphantly.
The habit is "generally low branched, with upright-
arching branches forming a rounded outline."
Like me, you might wonder about habit in this context.
Here it points to the tree's general architecture,

praised by Linnaeus for having "the most splendid
leaves and flowers named for the most splendid botanist,"
Pierre Magnol, by another French botanist,
Charles Plumier. A director of France's first botanical garden,
in Montpellier, Magnol might have never known a tree
was named in his honor. A matter of semantics:
we owe to him the use of the term *family*
to groups of plants resembling each other
as much, if not more, than the all-too-human members
of happy and unhappy families alike.

And if I visited the Jardin des Plantes
one quiet Sunday a few Julys ago when coping with a prognosis.
Concerning busts, nearly alone and surrounded
by formidable ones of Nostradamus, Rabelais, and others,
as well as a couple strolling about with a child.

I'd gone to the garden to calm my nervous system
and study the effects of varying shades of green
on my feelings' range of motion. A map on a sign
indicated I was at the heart of the garden:

> "Successively a testing ground under the great Magnol, a demonstration school...
> and then a systematic school... this sector was rehabilitated after World War II."

Amid the ghosts of plagues past, I found myself
producing scenarios of a dread fittingly gargantuan in scale.
Then and there, it dissolved at the sight of another
garden favorite with a daisy-like, heliotropic
disposition: radiating blanket flowers,
self-contained explosions of yellow-tipped orange
and, if you look closely, pink.

Under a *Magnolia grandiflora* a sign relayed
that, in 1689, Plumier had the idea of baptizing plants
discovered in America after the old continent's botanists.
A quarter century later he arrived at *magnolia* for a genus
predating bees and once coetaneous with dinosaurs.
Origin of the specimen: Southeastern US.
Longevity: "150 to 200 years."

    LES BEAUX ARBRES DU JARDIN DES PLANTES.

As for the one on Governors Island, this hybrid's
presence in North America is recorded as early as 1832.
Available for purchase at the Linnaean Botanic Garden
in Flushing, Queens, it was by far the costliest of the lot,
at $8 when most trees cost 50 cents. Here, its origin tale:

After fighting in Napoleon's armies
and "disabused of life's illusions," Soulange-Bodin,
for whom the saucer magnolia cultivar was named in 1826,
retired to his exotic nursery at a villa outside Paris.
An oft-quoted passage of his writings encapsulates the spirit
of his retreat:

> "To gardens I cheerfully devote the remainder of my life. I shall not retrace
> the sad picture of the past. The Germans have encamped in my garden. I have
> encamped in the gardens of the Germans. It had doubtless been better for both
> parties to have stayed home and planted their cabbages."

Cabbages being nothing like the hybrid he bred by extracting
pollen from *M. liliflora* blooms and dabbing it,
much like pigment, on the stigmatic surfaces
of *M. denudata*'s receptacles, streaking with purple
the so-called virginal purity of the latter's pallid tepals.
Thus, two species original to China merged in a French
culture the world found irresistible.

"*La culture! Que ce mot a de charmes et d'empire...*"
How much charm and empire the word *culture* has!

Information runs through these lines like sap,
leading to an inflorescence that's a terminal,
solitary flower.

Notice how the poem's aboutness became its burden.

How many other ways are there
to know trees.

AFTER THIS, BEGIN JUMPS

If a tree is a fact, is a copse a fact too?
A fact: chakras reluctant to open.
As Lucía said, "You get here, your channels close up.
You get there, they open up."
To enter you must go through the copse.
Abracadabra. Corpse, cadaver,
ábrete sésamo. Open sesame, remove
the stubborn block, the language constrained
at the glottis. Instead, shoot up from the crotch.
Zangoloteo mínimo, eléctrico.
Rattle the bifurcated trunk.
Bring not the split but the stream.
As per folk etymologies: Abracadabra.
"I will create as I speak."
Conscious as self as ever displayed, splayed
open, *ábrete sésamo.* An invocation.
A surface folds itself into a mouth.
Déjame hablar, aunque nadie me entienda.
Misunderstood because I'm neither verby nor nouny.
When you speak through scents, pheromones, toxins,
and electrical signals only, the arc is harder to follow.
They think we're out for ourselves only.
"*Vainas de ajonjolí que sólo con rozarse*
explotan y se abren."
For the mystic speaking a lingua ignota, *viriditas,*
the natural world's greenness, is divine
life's moisture, its sudor or sap.
Galinzia, her word for plane trees.

LONDON PLANE TREE

What empty chatter must they overhear
in the polluted habitats for which they're naturals.
The person on the nearby park bench
utters "Nicaragua" as if she wanted all to hear
her crisp Spanish pronunciation.
"Why do I... Why do my taxes have to cover
someone else's artificial insemination?"
"Why isn't it letting me go back?"
"There's an imbalance in your body, you have to figure it out. Are you looking
      at your phone too much before you go to bed?"
I came here to gauge whether Moses's
predilection for the London plane tree is justifiable
to the casual eye. I concur with him and also Jane:
"hardy, tough, lovely dappled shade..."
Unlike the silence of effigies, the silence of trees
 refuses to take sides in history's disputes.
Trunks and outspread branches caught mid-
motion in the process of letting the light in,
about to surpass their own reach as you look.
Specimens of all ages recently spotted

> standing outside my building (shopping bag snagged on a branch)
> flanking the landmarked street on the way to the neighborhood park
> enclosing the Theodore Roosevelt Park outside the Museum of Natural History
> delimiting Central Park, the United Nations, and Governors Island's quadrants
>   where they constitute 54% of the island's total leaf cover

"No two trees are exactly similar as I write this."
Exfoliating "cream, olive, light brown bark" blending with limestone
and brownstone and sandstone and brick and turning streets
into mirages. Into cinema. "Noble habit."

Leaves pointing every which way, bending the light,
giving it volume, suffusing the frame with a choreographic
spontaneity and splendor that makes up for the severity
of the grid. Camo hiding its mechanisms.

THE LOMBARD EFFECT

The scent of the forest
impregnating clothes
you brought to the country
overnight. The mystery
of its becoming
noticeable only after
you carried it on you
back to the city. As jarring
as the nightingale
that couldn't possibly
be making a racket
perched on the dense
fan-shaped boughs
of the American elm
near the building's
side entrance.

Electronica, car
alarm, covert anti-
loitering device?

Ill-suited vectors.

A musical repertoire
of over two-hundred songs
doesn't even secure breeding
rights. Half remain solo
and drained from the performance's exertion.
"The vociferous

song is of course
in complete opposition
to their observability,"
writes the engagement officer
of a conservation
charity for everyone
who cares about nature
across the pond.

In the quiet of the island's night are they less compelled to raise their pitch
and volume?

SYCAMORE: A LYRIC

Schirobuz   *Sicomoro*   *Sikomorea*

Tall and statuesque.

For the Druids, a sacred tree.

Three species are native to North America.

Tuning starts fresh.

Beginnings fork new.

Tuning forks.

Backscratchers tickling the atmosphere.

Phantom limbs.

Winged seeds.

Sap, medicinal.

Leaves warding off evil spirits. Bad energy.

Ghost of the forest.

Ghost of an emblem chopped down for the sake of it, a sentinel at Hadrian's Wall.

"Does it need more phantom?"

That's the inner dialogue of a sound person dealing with noise.

"Phantom power on."

REMOTE DISJUNCTIONS

I didn't mind ferns enough, I thought, the last time I hiked up
to Lookout Point. They're so unassuming. I'd be looking
at the tops of third-generation redwoods, or beyond, toward
Googleplex, in Mountain View, which later Google confirmed
was the complex off in the distance. And I'd be picturing,
those last days, rhizomes and spores. Sorry to make you feel judged,
I almost texted. Stopped myself. Truth is I judge, and if judges
were prone to feeling sorry, they wouldn't. I welcomed noise
instead of trying to block it out with the folk musician's songs,
Scottish, coming from my laptop. If you don't remember a name,
does it mean you don't care to remember. You'd taken yourself
to places whose specifics you'd chosen to forget. You said you
weren't there to keep track, but to experience. Which, when
I'm feeling negative, I translate as ditching the thing as soon as
you're done with it onto the heap of junk you're not accumulating.
Those who get the backend know what detailed tagging can lead to:
a map so precise it's the territory's size. We're drifting apart
again, spore-like. I'm done completing your sentences.
A version of the signs along the trail anticipating the hikers'
ups and downs. "It begins with feeling," was the first, spotted
at the same time I noticed the pet waste bags someone had left
behind. "Here you leave your worries," seen after I passed a guy
whose grin was such, he did seem to have just dumped them.
This one got me thinking about our tendency to ruin things:
"This is a beautiful moment." The last wasn't part of the art:
"Please keep out of area under renovation." That resonated.

THEN AGAIN

an impulse, pastoral
returning
on the trail
gaze seesawing
what eye
saw was
the ease
of a leaf
gliding
off an oak tree
slicing the air
butterflies
hide-and-seek
forewings
eyespots
hindwings
duplicated fluttering
in a figure eight
pattern, traces
of material-
ized light,
eye fooled

***

PHANTOM

Skirt the mind's traps, the mind
being. A parabola. I go outside,
look up at the half-full moon that is a quarter
moon—half of a half visible, other half turned
away in perpetuity. How unlike me. The celestial.
The other one, turned off by the drive
towards an aesthetic object. Unclear
if what repels is the becoming
object or the becoming art.
Will you quit it with your all or nothing.
The poem I entertain under the quarter moon
looking like a half-full moon refuses
to come back inside with me.
To find its stead I search for merism.

DISTANCE CALCULATOR

I. Take the width of a border between two spaces
and split it by as many places the border divides.
Repeat as many times as necessary to arrive at zero.

2. Eyeball how many clouds there could be in the sky
at any given moment, then count them.
Compare the number of clouds you thought you were seeing
with the number of clouds you were able to count.
Multiply the difference by the time you spent looking upward.
The resulting number equals a unit of distance in clouds.

3. For an estimate of the distance between a point
within any of the nations on the planet still using the imperial system
and any other point outside, multiply
the numerical difference between in and cm
by that between ft and m, by that between mi and km.
Then multiply that figure by the distance
between point A and point B, times two.

4. With a cord six times longer than the possible responses
to a multiple option question
with no adequate choices for you to check.

5. Gauge the temporal and spatial intervals between
being at the right place at the right time and being
at the wrong place at the wrong time.
Quantify in units of gratitude or regret
depending on the situation.

SUNSTEAD

Amid a few nonplussed party guests,
to contemplate Emilie's astounding-
ly inventive dresses for survival in
adversity, dresses that grow food,
float, and provide seating and shelter.
Self-irrigating dresses, plaid and inflatable
dresses with hooks, storage pouches,
and foam extensions. Twelve days later
"hell itself breathes out contagion
to this world" with an unfathomable
267,000 daily infections nationally.
It gets worse. Dense brain
can't grasp the radiant clusters, the kinetics
of the fifteenth letter of the alphabet.
"It's all Greek to me." Going bust too,
another high-end clothing retailer joins
the experience economy, rebrands
itself as a purveyor of experiences
in Copenhagen sometime down the line
when experience can be experienced again.
Duck face will have to do for the time being.
Some don beaks in floral patterns or animal
prints, with Mickey Mouse on them, logos,
slogans, and even sequined beaks,
while others continue to refuse them.

It's the longest night of the year.

Tin tree ornaments from Sueños Inc.
come at Leo's behest when showing him
our tree on a live video call

TORTUGA   ELEFANTE   COCODRILO   TIGRE   LEÓN

At two he skips four when counting to five—
that I didn't get the turtle and the tiger
goes unnoticed. In their stead came a serpent
and a bull and a giant red pepper to write
in signs that a toddler might understand.
Never mind the bull's bullfighting attire.

Time is either ripe for undoing, unripe
for the doing, or all of the above.

It's the longest night of the year.

AHÍ VIENE EL LOBO

The old approach captured
by "The only good wolf
is a dead wolf" adage. Now
captivity increases the odds
of its survival. Outlasted by forever
stamps commemorating legal
provisions—or rather, the lobo's
will to defy its endangered status.
Life span of six to eight years
in the wild. Numbers so low
its howling has to go further
in maintaining the pack.
I was wrong in thinking just
malignancies could be extirpated.
Fatalism will only take us so far;
as it turns out, they're still viable
in a territory larger than previously
calculated. The presumption
that their diet was unadaptable
to dwindling populations of prey
(ungulates, rabbits, small mammals)
led to erroneous assessment of the suitability
of various terrains. Causes for the shrinking
of their natural range include cattle
ranchers' proverbial hostility
but not environmental destruction.
Add division between agencies north
and south of a border proved arbitrary
by the very continuity of habitats

for countless species on either side,

the Mexican gray wolf one among many.

Once the stuff of legend: *Lobo*

Lobo your name will survive

for no man could bring you in dead or alive!

Now its "majestic beauty"

graces correspondence no

doubt traveling more widely.

DECEMBER

Who can say where we're going. To be sure
I'd split my attention so now looking
back. I couldn't tell. If I'd succumbed to the logic
of the gimmick when breaking. Things
to "make the stone stonier"
when even the scare. Not a cliché.
Quotes demanded to be in quotes.
When the numbness setting in was as frightening
a prospect. There was something to be said
about technique. Like the technology of looking
away from one screen to have the eyes
land in a scene from a music video on mute
on another screen. false no show priority style parent margin pagination widow
        orphan font family theme minor latin, seen.
Code visible all of a sudden, scrambling
everything like malware or virus. In that frame
an extravaganza of go-go boots, a Dolly-ish queen and a cowboy
leaning on a horse pen's fence, all glam
color saturation and radiance. What I'd wanted here
was to place a comma, take a breather, retrace
my steps, but we jumped into the New Year sitting
down, broadcasting ourselves rapt not wondering how.
We ended up here in other corners of the web where delusion
kept up its recruitment of denialists denying denial strategy
or tactic the question unanswerable even
in hindsight. A line for each day of the month
reminding me of Katalin Ladik's saying only
in performance does she figure out what her scores mean.

Later we'd know that the actions to "settle the score"
were no improvisation so I ascribed them
to a time prior to their having happened, would they,
like the truthism that was once an oft-told lie, repeat again.

FIT TO PRINT

Late in November appears a variant of concern. The news gets torn up. The room is also a house in the immersive tests and rioting. The houses you definitely don't want include a deepening political divide. Not guilty of homicide a counterfactual fable in a case that ignited man and her family. Able to maintain the definition most strikingly that he had acted across generations. Partial lunar eclipse when first woman becomes acting president for 85 minutes. Full bright moon had become stiffer. The pictures could be splendor. Multiple moon and sun disorders of fracture. Last year "has healed nicely." Tuesday will be a career out of being. You will unfold as a flow. Clouds and sunshine mild-mannered. Few clueless skies and the wind turbulent. Wednesday will rage at those celebrating the cold. The high verdict over a slogan associated with his medic bag. The jurors could set off the unrest.

"Don't let any frescos give in to climate change."

"We hope that eats away at you for a long time."

"Harm that is truly crazy uses the most states," she said, sanctioning illegal choices out there.

NOT AGAINST THE RULES

It hailed golf balls
back in June.

Notebook got nicked,
got soaked.

What month is it.

She speaks
of grief so gracefully
you hold on to her words
lest you miss
its gnawing at you too.

Daily broadcasts
of an unimaginable assortment
of newly weaponized
subjects.

Fragments of him
were residue. Counter-
texts.

I am writing in the dark
and that is what the noise is about.

SYSTEM BEGINS TO COLLAPSE, EVEN

"Let's start at the top. My hands are tied," the candidate mutters. The barrier is planned to pass through astrocytes that nurture neurons so they can keep working properly. The watchdog group questions why the photographers were early to document the incursion. Were they recycling old images to make a new point with the goal of tilting the public narrative, they ask. A councilwoman is seen observing a protest with the butt end of a firearm protruding from a far more mysterious half. Steel bollards stacked near a cemetery are an ominous sign of zip ties.

"In two different worlds, separated by airplanes and oceans in lands that attract migratory birds along with birding tourists—how can it be affecting us here?" The question reverberates, while fertilizer is becoming unaffordable, diminishing harvests and, with new technologies, human brain cells from biopsied tissue or cadavers are collected by robots at the brain atlas.

"The shelling is not stopping."

She surrenders her Smith & Wesson 9-millimeter pistol and her permit but does not respond to a text message seeking comment. Envelopes full of claims and counterclaims based on doctored images and misinformation spread out. People turn to sources that mirror their feelings. Having identified more than 3,300 types of cells, microglia keep attacking foreign invaders and pruning branches to improve chemical and electric signaling. Likability notes come from on high as soon as a complex character is on the page suggesting a double standard.

"We want to know what the orchestra is doing," he said. "At this moment in time no one cares what this one violinist is doing."

FLIP SIDE

Transmissions paused temporarily in certain regions of the planet.
No marks made it to the page then, hence the retroactive declaratives.
If you looked up at the yellow dwarf star at the right time in the right place,
you'd see the culprits, sunspots, sitting there available to the naked eye
and readily confused with muscae volitantes, a.k.a. floaters, where loops
of magnetic field in the sun's photosphere find their footpoints and launch
themselves out to its atmosphere—its corona—tracing arcs of light
so beauteous their optimization as screensavers is likely a fait accompli.
Set them to Vangelis and they make for even better ambience. The sun's
on its twentieth cycle, lasting eleven years and manifesting as alternating bouts
of languor and hyperactivity visible in the number of blemishes. News
has it that in late October the sun had an outburst, hurling plasma
and highly energetic particles our way. Its mass ejection supercharged
the northern lights I've never seen and caused a brief radio blackout across
Earth's daylit side, centered somewhere in the South American vastness.
Whether it all connects or this is another instance of word magic falls beyond
this account's purview, this side of paranormal. Face the sun.

Close your eyes. What do you see.

DID YOU ACCIDENTALLY SUMMON ME?

Out with Shadow, at the crossroad
listening to the Wilson podcast on how
to translate death imagery
in the *Iliad*—the freeing of limbs,
as if one's body parts were tied
in a knot that death loosens
upon striking. A truck
dashes by advertising
interior demolition.

Most encounters now chance-
determined.

                    If this note were to ever reach
                    you, please forgive my scream
                    when you bumped into me while
                    fooling around with the other kids
           at the park. "Tag, you're it!" You weren't
                    out to give me the disease.
                    Your laughter, carefree, my "niña,
                    ¡pon atención!" terrifying you,
                    built-up panic and rage unleashed,
                    voice turned menacing extremity.

                    If you choose not to it's only fair.

WORD SCRAMBLER

In the summer of 2019, after commuting to and fro from the city to Providence to the city and elsewhere for a few years, I settle back in New York and plan to recruit friends to write a collaborative novella. Each participant must first propose that we do something together. It can be anything, from hosting a listening session to doing something we've never done before, like going fishing in the East River, picking a subway line and exploring the areas around each one of its stops, kayaking to Ellis Island, touring monuments in the five boroughs, going to a silent disco, or sneaking into a convention at the Jarvis Center. Our experience will be the basis of each chapter. The novella will be a love letter to the city that is home to many of the people I love. Summer goes by too fast. I run out of time while trying to finish a book on repetition. I'll get to it next year, I figure.

In the summer of 2020, I watch *Palm Springs*—a sci-fi film that's somewhat of a remake of *Groundhog Day*. The lead character is stuck in a time loop and wakes up to the same day over and over again, readying himself to attend the same wedding each time 'round. His behavior changes every iteration of the main plot, but nothing has consequences since whatever has happened during the day erases itself at night and the present keeps rebooting to the same day. Awareness of his entrapment is his freedom. I write this in an email to someone who's asked how my summer went, but I take it out before pressing send since I'm not sure exactly what I am relaying. The question remains open: Did I advance my learning of helplessness or did I teach myself to resist it in 92 days? For what it's worth, I realize that by adding fifteen words to this paragraph I can match the count of the one above.

OBVERSE

The fear is that this pause once again is the general slowdown before traffic comes
to a halt indefinitely. Everyone at one with their pace before slamming on
the breaks almost too late, as when the connection is unstable and syllables
elongate, compress and jumble on top of each other in transmission and
you keep going regardless, saying to yourself, To hell with technology, I am
just gathering speed, my thoughts finally crystallized into something worth
saying. Just then you freeze mid-motion in the most awkward of gestures,
mouth ajar, hands gesticulating. You lost the connection, no one heard what
you said, not even the screen registered. You're in a slight panic trying to
reconnect before you lose everyone for good and find yourself alone again
with your thoughts. A little like Aunt Melita did before she died in a steam
room in Cuernavaca, though at the time of the fatal stroke the warm mist
took her in its lulling embrace.

Where am I when I am elsewhere and in this room, revisiting pictures of an
overdue family reunion.

Posing for selfies we see each other seeing each other on the screen, our gazes'
feedback loops bathing us in love hormone's glow.

Leo sending you kisses, Jenny peeking from behind with her wide eyes looking
into the depths of Mexican soil, by which I mean their synecdoche.

Acapulco with its sunsets invariably postcard-like, especially from the vantage
of one of the Northeast's wettest Augusts on record.

Where my device turns the setting sun into a flying saucer taking me back.

Where Mile tells stories of her great-grandfather's arrival on the shores of the

Atlantic, prompting my father to quote a former president's appreciation of immigrants from Lebanon: "Whomever doesn't have a Lebanese friend, go find one!"

Where a gurgling Nico stretches the length of my thighs, gauging the strength of his grip by clenching my fingers while locking eyes with mine. What does he see as I plunge into his gaze outside language?

Let that be the pause.

Let time stop where sunbeams crack open the skies, streaking clouds with iridescence and blazing oranges, turning them into spiderwort-pink landscapes mirroring the lapping waves. The open sky another picture of an interior, its dynamics harmonized, cloud formations coalescing into shapes whose significance eludes you as soon as you begin spelling them out.

My father and I with sunspots that will eventually match. The source of his dimpled smile beyond the frame; his focus turned inward, retrospective.

Dorothy on a night drive to the Acapulco of a bygone era in search of her late grandmother's house near the cliffs of La Quebrada, world-famous for its divers, near Playa Langosta. Was the beach narrow or lobster-shaped?

Her nostalgia rhymes with mine as I try to locate the place we stayed at the summer I donned an Olivia Newton-John headband wanting "to get physical" before a surgery.

These are my pictures, not my disclosures. We're nearing code red and sheltering in a place not big enough for all of those in all of us.

Cathy's lashes augmenting her awe of her little ones that matches my awe of her. Once I wondered who she'd be in the future that is the photo's now.

What astounds, is it our age difference or the speed at which her visions materialize.

Write this or unlive. Memory's future or its undoing.

Leo sings Joplin's "The Entertainer" whose glossolalic lyrics are made up of the word *mañamañamaña*. Sure of what he's saying, it's his version of *mañana* maybe, an untranslatable. Once he's on the other side of language he will have forgotten it.

Santiago, manga-entranced and learning Japanese, awake when we sleep and silent when we talk except for when he thanks us for his meals from a place on the same coordinates as ours.

Ernesto spending hours in the ocean uninterrupted and thus hard to take photos of. It's the Pisces in him. Green eyes say one thing, mouth says another. Both buoyant.

I lose my spot and revisit the pictures again, dragging the past into the now, palliative for present wants.

My mother, betrayed sunworshipper who sat outside unprotected for too long. I can barely see her in the backlit snapshot of her sunbathing in the bay on the other side of Punta Diamante back in the 1970s, when she's a still a recent transplant from the East Coast.

Time's obverse.

Write this or unlive. Memory's undoing or its future.

Playeros pihuihuí, sandpipers everywhere, undisturbed by my presence as they stand near the surf like families with kiddies wading at the beach.

Not photographed: trash on the sand. Styrofoam bits, plastics, bottle caps, wrappers. Cigarette butts, masks. Abandoned palapas and half-finished resorts near the derelict property of Luis Miguel, the pop star gone bankrupt. People and their dogs breaking in. Faux cement rocks. Construction sites nearby, a luxury building in the shape of an eye, curved futuristic façade surrounded by palm trees here and there. Quad bikes everywhere on the beach, fuel scent wafting in the sea breeze.

Adolfo turned image, standing on the surf and gripping bartered wild caught fish in each hand.

Mikaela in the same band tee-shirt I'll later see another teenager wearing on the NYC subway. Psychedelic sun. She knows the quad bike's name, *cuatrimotos*, her young poet eyes sensing too that this jumble of experiences discarded as material is the future. Too personal for me, for her not personal enough.

A dead *tecolote* washed up on the sand with hollowed out owl eyes. Petrified, a child stumbles on it minutes before me. Shocked from the sight, I mumble "Pobre búho" to nobody in particular.

Later there are other owls, one painted, a baptism gift, and three stone ones keeping watch at a nearby brownstone back home in Queens, where a tropical storm pauses to make a clearing for a blue moon to appear.

On this same day, my mother reminds me I was born one month and two days after man's first steps on the moon. She later leaves me another message saying she gets it, "the flowers and phone calls are nice but of course your birthday always brings you back to where you started."

"An Aztec century ago, incidentally," I say, again, to nobody in particular.

The following day and a half brings two months' worth of rainfall. The phrase "explosive intensification" doesn't mean anything to me yet.

THAT AUGUST

We leave town on and off
and off and on. The plants
seem hardier for it, as if they too
needed space. The compulsoriness of
our uninterrupted company sucks
the air out of the room, pollutes
their habitat. As if they too sensed
the pulsations of our reluctance.
Five more days pass. In that corner
of the sky, Orion is the constellation
whose pinholes I point out to Jane.
Shadow prances as we walk
over to a darker area of the field
to catch the shooting stars. The sadness
of the turn the poem took takes us
by surprise. We find ourselves
welling up. Verbing. We lose
our grip. Once, to love the city,
you had to hate it every now and
again; disappointment preordained
by expectation of returns. There's
intermittent eroticism, the erotics
of intermittence, and dead ends.
Andy says he's gone for good.
Aki and Makiko head back to Japan.
Neighbors leave for the suburbs.
Even Angela, born and bred
in the East Village, wants out.
The skyline discontinues itself at night

but sidewalk furniture doesn't go unwanted.
We rarely visited the joint down the street—
menu board blank, awning still there.
At the park, a man goes on in disbelief
about a Staten Islander who's not once
set foot in Central Park. Across the river
we get stuck in traffic on 42nd. A truck
driver keeps his cool, plays a flute
between lights. The wax museum's
reopened. Minnie takes a breather, mouse
mask dangling from neck, face mask
over nose and mouth. Another
river over, American Dream,
a mammoth new complex,
remains empty in Jersey.

THEOREM OF SORTS

We admire adults for not acting like children,
meaning we don't have to clean up after them,
while we spend at least half of a life trying
to find ways to exceed the edges
of shapes that cannot be found.

At the dinner table he brings up the guy
who "does these beautiful magical dioramas,"
micro-grated Parmesan cheese dangling
from the dinged edge of a bowl covered in oil.

Later that week folding pages at the art school
keeps us occupied. Notes are taken and much is said
while repetition begins fielding itself.
What kind of bird chirps potato chips?

Here the most common sightings are of
American goldfinches and cardinals,
migratory and nonmigratory respectively,
the latter mostly male and so territorial
they'll attack their own reflection on occasion.

You won't find the difference between a peaceful being
and being peaceful on differencebetween.net.
Other approaches are requisite, body scans.
If your heartbeat can't be found under the medical gown
the shutdown's become emotional for you.

This is the likely end to a year we want
to forget or the one forgetting itself as it is coming
to an end. Except that it isn't, ongoingness
has its way of "keeping on keeping on," not even
when it all stops, since the so-called ending folds itself
into the ever-developing story, begging the question,
is it airless, the POV? Who sees the narrator?
Is this relatable and on whose terms?

The proposal involves switching mediums.
I will play a faculty member at the art school
on whose faculty I am serving, folding
myself as a fictional character into a true story.

In the vicinity, the charm of hummingbirds,
murder of crows, and identity taxation.

Repetition fielding itself again, reading
against icons. A flexible field trip to nowhere.

When one painter speaks to another painter, I know
that to be fully in this won't ever be available to me either,
since none of us are exhibitionists.

The poem speaks in signs and the painting
on velvet sucks the light out of the room,
yet somehow we manage to communicate.

As for the empty speech bubbles on the walls,
they display a variety of shapes, all very talkative.

CLOSET DRAMA

CEILING (*looking down at PERSON on the floor*): Why are you playing corpse?

WALLS (*to each other*): She stares at us interchangeably when she tires of glaring at the hopelessly pathetic advertising across the street.

CEILING (*to WINDOWS*): Illegible from this vantage. What is it?

WINDOWS: "Live Well, Forge Ahead." A state of mind, a way of life.

COLUMN: Plus details about available square footage.

CORNER 1: I'm fortunate to be spared such sight. Last thing I need right now is motivation from real-estate developers.

WINDOWS (*to all CORNERS*): Say that to your angling of shadows.

CORNER 2: All I ever see outside are stacks of windows across the street and scaffolding coming down at a painfully slow rate, at glacial speed.

COLUMN: "A New York point of view."

PERSON: Glacial? You need an idiom upgrade! At the rate glaciers are melting now, you would've seen the scaffolding come down way before the contagion began.

(*No part of the room wants to hear they're passé. Cabin-feverish themselves, they become more animated when hearing Bad Bunny from a passing car's booming sound system.*)

CORNER 3 (*to PERSON*): Why don't you replay your temporary savior complex instead of getting on our case?

WALLS: Besides doodles, the papers on the table contain notes on hypervigilance and the displacement of experience.

COLUMN (*twisting*): What is it: outside looking in, inside looking out? Outside looking down, inside looking up?

CEILING (*to PERSON*): Let me repeat the question. Why are you playing corpse?

PERSON (*chanting*):

These days, walks are my cinéma vérité.
I socialize in my dreams.
I climb the social ladder up and down in my dreams.
Dreams are my social nightmare, my cinéma vérité.

Walks are my party. My cinéma vérité. *Namaste.*

FLOORBOARDS (*in unison*): She was a visitor quote unquote.

THAT JULY

On the day of national
incongruity memorializing
the misalignment of universals
with particulars, instead of fireworks
two boulders on the sidewalk
painted institutional green—
hostile architecture, barriers
flanking the lobby of a building
on a boulevard named for the "King
of Greenpoint" (double standards
or an impossibility theorem
for clustering)—garner a snapshot.

So does a balloon of the same color rising
above the mourning crowd
assembled at the park listening
to passages by Frederick Douglass
read in relays: "To him,
your celebration is a sham."
A girl in a skirt the same
green faces the camera.

Later another portrait takes the form
of fortune cookies piled into a room's corner
and the maxim "There is no glory
unless you put yourself on the line"
as if delivered by Felix Gonzalez-Torres
in this unerotic version of Pandemos—

our commonality the distance
between us, the pathology
of our entanglement.

PROMPT

They turn the tables on me and give me an assignment: to write in the voice of
an armed protester.

The more strident the voices, the more they merge together.

"It's weird to think that this all started with an off-the-cuff rant over Aladdin the
musical.

Heil Witmer! (sic)

She's the reason we need the 2nd amendment.

Fuck you, fake news. Put me on TV too. My name is Fred, I'll give you my card.

Six feet. Yeah. Fuck you.

I've got hydroxychloroquine, I'm fine.

I've slipped a noose around my brown-haired Barbie doll's neck.

'Western chauvinist' includes all races, religions, and sexual preferences.

We refuse to apologize. We're not the alt-right.

Being proud of Western culture today is like being a _____ , _____ , _____
communist in 1953.

Michigan Proud Boys USA

U R A JOKE !! If you were born a woman and would like to be involved, there is a
girls (sic) group. They call themselves Proud Boys' Girls.

TYRANT BITCH."

I tell them that this is the type of language that cannot be unheard.

I tell them I'm afraid I am being reductive by trying to clear the air and wonder if I sound like a motivational speaker.

I don't tell them that these types of "denials and discrepancies" are not unlike the type described by Javier Marías in *Bad Nature, or with Elvis in Mexico* as accumulating and coexisting with what they refute, be it true or false. Those that "never cancel anything out but only end up sanctioning it for as long as people go on talking, the only way to erase is to say nothing..."

I don't tell them that Marías's story about the King in Acapulco is apocryphal but they can watch him mangle Spanish on YouTube.

No one brings up Burroughs's notion of language as virus or the virulence of certain discourses, let alone inoculation strategies.

Chekhov's gun goes unmentioned too.

PRIORITY WAS HANDWRITTEN

So I bit my tongue.
Looked up "how to cure
mouth sores" again in the span
of a week. The body trying to tell
me something I refuse
to accept cogniti-
vely. *Naïveté* a word negating
what it means, spoken
in reference to a third one. Bit
myself while chewing a bar of some-
thing eaten in lieu of a meal,
of the hard and crunch-
y variety
associated by some with
anger. I had wanted to rid myself
of the bad taste in my mouth. Hearing
the voices in your head
as sanity's only
safeguard. Alice, I felt
you were talking to me when
reading, "But you have never
really been in love,"
and she was saying yes,
yes, once, I was, am I?
I fell once, but in Spanish
nunca caí al amor. Cliché,
also from the French, I
don't really speak; since my mouth
lacks come-hither pronouncing

lips, the invitation failed
to materialize. There is language
equality and linguistic equivalence;
they are not interchangeable with each other.
"Absentee" was the song playing
while I read *"La cara no es el espejo*
del alma.... La máscara está vacía.
Habla sin lengua."
Tongueless speech,
no one behind the mask.

APRIL

What you stand
up for, that's
precisely the elision.
Press share post
sitting still. Break
this up where
you will, I
don't care. If
love matches like,
brings the simulation
of attention, its
cacophony. Right then,
music being her
fuel, thoughts of
Ana burst into
the poem. Last
name unknown. Our
community, more provisional
than we'd anticipated,
the dance entertained
as if to
treat thinking as
an experimental field
of action. Her
words, their source,
her bonds, as
factual as dust
gathering every other
week, cherry tomatoes

from a garden
upstairs, her preexisting
condition. Her humor,
knowing, her infection.
No glimmer of
her eyes in
the numbers dissolving.
Stings, to know
her not. Her
not being anymore.
Her gone. Blooming
three short-lived
blooms thrice, the
walking iris, spring
she didn't partake
of lingering on.

TRIPLE TURN AND SKIP

es marzo marzo es
marzo es marcha
es amarse es marte de la guerra dios
a marte es amarte y es marcha
marchan los días y la lucha
sí la lucha sigue sí hay círculos
que nunca se cierran círculos que se cierran
círculos que se cierran círculos que nunca se cierran
hay círculos círculos y círculos semicírculos o circunferencias incompletas
hay círculos que son círculos que son ondas en lo menos hondo
de las superficies líquidas que son olas y círculos que son ondas sonoras
círculos sonidos que son idos o son nidos
hay círculos que son nidos y hay círculos que son idos
continuándose en círculo en espiral
los círculos nunca se cierran
continuándose en círculo en espiral
los círculos

RETURN TO PSYCHOGEOGRAPHY

Funny, I wasn't thinking of communicating in a language other than this one, but here I am. Feeling formally restless and leaving traces.

I can't get into it right now, so I'll switch back and forth, if it's okay.

In the spirit of the diagrammatic, sitting maskless under a blooming tree at a coffee shop.

Not a European copper beech. There's no room for such majesty in this enchanted catastrophe.

He was speaking about the words' disobedience, about how poets work by not working. Meanwhile the world's machinery was running its course.

When even shadows peter out.

The possible end words in a looping poem all related to nutrient broths, nanoparticles, and mRNA. Not surprisingly it ended up turning into an unfinished anti-sestina.

Before February's disorientation there were family pictures in November.

You were shown the future of fitness on mirror.com.

As with all mirror reflections, the image was flipped—a translation.

The future's only visible in hindsight.

No, not last night. In the afternoon, when she warned us that things would be getting intense.

The lightbox announced a "trend watch" in all caps. Under it, the same unhoused woman from last night, her belongings in plastic bags spread out around her.

The underground is the only true measure of the grid.

Another incident derails the day again.

Describe the incident.

An occurrence of an action or situation that is a separate unit of experience.

So it takes you out of the flow?

Something like that, yes, although it is actually woven deeply into the day's fabric, but still manages to feel isolated from everything, unlike a current.

What's your currency?

No crisis.

Is that the cruel optimist in you speaking?

Absurd. What's for breakfast?

I take care of you. It's a sign of respect.

Unrequited.

Mutually so.

Bad better than best. That's what Rodrigo had suggested.

The reference to Beckett was obvious; still, he thought the connection was brilliant.

Quería que me volviera más mala.

When John spoke of Rodrigo I thought of peacocks.

That makes two Rodrigos then.

Me lo dijo un pajarito. A little birdie told me, back when birds of the resplendent type could talk.

Epic commute, and still the continuous loop of the present.

Such were my nonmusical subtitles for Richard's *Psalms for the End of the World*.

Ninety more seconds to go.

THAT MARCH

A glove is no banana peel
on the sidewalk.
Uncoupled or twinned, sighted
often. Recumbent,
released by the hand's reach.

Signaling to passersby,
left behind, discarded—either
way, overlooked. Speaking
gestures of waste, how we protect
ourselves. One becomes many,
spreads.

Nitrile among utility
markings, masks, trash, in lots,
parks, amid shopping carts and hieroglyphs
in a different key, stains.
Ghostly ciphers of fear.

Mimes in a minimal choreography
of absence. Dormant,
thought infected. Fallen
blossoms, mock
birds.

MOVEMENT PHRASES

With nothing to look forward to, disorientation   ensues. I am not one to
plan   my next move standing still.   I need to be on my way before I
know   where I am going. I think with my fingers,   to quote someone
else who's miles ahead.

Fingers, legs—I am using them indistinctly   here, for nothing comes to
mind   until I leave the house and walk   to the waterfront park about a
mile and a quarter away.   The sun has set already. Across the river   the
West Side twinkles in a crimson light.   I walk to the Newtown Creek
into which, a few months later,   a Greenpoint old-timer will throw police
barricades   protesting the Open Streets program   that shuts traffic on
certain blocks, alleging   it only benefits the neighborhood's hipsters.

Once at the creek, a tributary   of the East River doubling as a Superfund
site,   I realize that the building I orient myself with,   vacated by
Citibank in the last year and once the tallest in the area,   now displays the
name of a corporation   I've never heard of. It happens to be   exactly
in the direction opposite   to where I expected it to be.   Triangles, not
squares,   dominate this part of the borough.

I walk toward the building instead of retracing   my steps through the
park. A bank as polestar is wrong but not new.   It features prominently in
the Queens Plaza station's tile mural   reproducing the exact topography of
the area above the station   circa 2005, *Look Up, Not Down*.   The artist,
Ellen Harvey, could've designed the murals for people   to make sure that
when they emerge from the underworld   back to street level, they do so
on the right side   of the chaotic juncture outside.   The street names at
the exits of the station being   insufficient given the local grid's   idiosyn-
crasy: the same number designates an avenue,   a street, a road, a place, a

lane,   and a drive and the logic   underlying the system appears
unintelligible, as if conceived   to gaslight visitors to the borough.   As
if the city planners   who found a way to squeeze more roads   into
the grid without having to revise the numbering system   already in place
in the 1900s   also sought to prove Zeno's paradox   on the nominal
impossibility   of movement from point A   to point B.

Before long I know where   I am. I pass the beer hall I never made it to:
for rent now.   I make a left at the end of Vernon Avenue, at the intersection
with Jackson.   I know every block of Jackson Avenue   so well it doesn't
matter   that I'm not wearing my glasses. The fog   from the mask would
be more of an inconvenience   than my nearsightedness anyway. I pass
Manducatis,   a red-sauce eatery empty tonight   except for the perpet-
ually present manager   whose suit and demeanor matches a mortician's.
He's doing accounting alongside a giant Rolodex on a table near the window.
Every time   we'd pass a cemetery, my late grandfather   would crack
the same joke: "That place is so popular,   people are dying to get in
there."   Not that it applies to this place   always half empty, as if the
sparse patrons seen through   the lace curtains were the Old Country's
ghosts,   long gone.

Ghosts of the before times   flash before my eyes. Ghosts of those who
departed not knowing   a calamity of this magnitude   could ever befall
the planet. The untimely   ghosts of those who took their own lives   or
were taken away by fluke accidents, cancer, overdoses, heartbreaks,
breakdowns.   I hear Aura's perfect-pitch impressions of Nico   at a bar
in Coney Island   one summer in, what was it, 2003, 2004   *When you're
all alone and lonely   in your midnight hour* Lou Reed sings   and the
waves of the Atlantic lap at our feet   on our tipsy way back to the car.
We're at Andrew's for dinner across from Bowie's place   on Lafayette.
Never had a sighting.   I see Juan in the railroad apartment on Bank Street
whose lease he later passed on to me.   Anne and I at the wine bar on
Vernon   straight out of a noir film.   I've yet to return.

C.D. crammed into a corner after dancing to Amy Winehouse   at
Barbara's birthday/New Year's Eve bash   in the West Village   the night
midnight struck while we were underground   and so we reveled with
fellow riders   until we got to our stop.   Carolee at Rio Mar in the Meat-
packing District   on one of the first times we hung out.   Carla and I
seeing the *Radical Women* show   at the Brooklyn Museum, which Carolee
and she could've been in   were it not for Carla's being too young   and
for Carolee's not being Latin American.

Once this was the city of serendipity.   The algorithm chooses as accom-
paniment Robert Wyatt's "At Last I Am Free"   *I can hardly see in front of
me...*   Nothing to look forward to   but people in boxes. It is February.
The streets are dead.

PRETEND IT'S A MOVIE (LAST JANUARY)

There is Z again, in a park bench
near the playground and dog run,
as if waiting for me. *As if* because
she's pretending not to but is.
Delays with the paperwork mean
no groceries for her today.
She needs shoes. Men's shoes.
Minutes later, a pair materializes
on the concrete chess table near us.
She has God's ear. In my mouth
again the taste of awkwardness,
as if I'd meant my saying, "I'm here
to help you." As if I were pretending
to be looking for her and am. As if
she meant her saying she would
pay me back sometime. "Don't
be silly," I say, not meaning it either;
she doesn't do silly. What is
and what isn't the case. The world
according to an I speaking about you
with whom mutuality is possible
only in fleeting exchanges. She here
relegated to the third person, who
improbably trusts me as much as I
trust her, which isn't saying much.
The construction triply negative.
In a hurry I once dodged her
to avoid the unease of having

to leave—my self-importance.
Our reperformances staged
in a four-block radius, movements
synchronized like those of Shadow
and I whom she complimented
breaking the ice. We're aware
of gaps and they pain us differently.
People want stories that illustrate
their bridging, or its illusion.
Here this does not happen. Today
I left the house wanting to ask
what story she'd like me to write about her.
The story's that good, someone beat me to it,
you say. Besides, I'd have to pay for it.
You weave together a birth in Tibet,
an abduction, a supreme court judge,
the priest of the church down the street,
Barack Obama, a rape, a murder attempt,
a cover-up, a $29 million settlement, and
just when it's inconceivable there'd be more
to add, you mention a forced sex alteration
confirmed by doctors upon finding your
dick in your stomach. You're playing me,
which in my idiom means you're seeing
my face. You call me María.
You still have God's ear.
You don't mention housing
vouchers, your neighbor's outrage,
your empty fridge.
"Love you," is how you say goodbye.
"Love you too," I mutter as Shadow
pulls me back to our square.

A YEAR AND A DAY

All verb, no subject.

An anti-pastoral that forgets to forget that poetry is underwritten by labor.

An odd triangulation between us.

And blueberries in the bushes, if you look.

At some point he asks me if I still have the ring he once gave me. He needs it back.

Black squares: analog, digital.

Bruce asleep. He may or may not be dreaming and rarely remembers his dreams.

Cathy & Adolfo asleep in the living room. They may or may not be dreaming.

Carla visits me in the dream. She's alive and uncharacteristically cheerful.

Covid not in the picture.

Cumbia at the taco stand in the market.

Ghostly campuses downtown.

Going on being.

I closed my eyes and saw ripples in the Sea of Tranquility.

I don't think I would like him if we met at a party—feelings of intense dislike.

I dream a reversal: I had this unquenchable thirst and my father confronted me about my drinking.

I get on a crowded bus that makes a long stop in front of Woodhull Hospital.

I need to keep the door open.

I'd shut myself in my office, but there's no ventilation in here.

I'm here to write down this line by William James: the "great thing in all education is to make our nervous system our ally instead of our enemy."

"If you're bored give it up."

In the dream, I say to someone that of course it'd make sense that I'm having trouble sleeping, who isn't, given what we're all reading and seeing on the news.

I was coming from a building I've never been to that often appears in other dreams.

It's the first Saturday in March.

It's the start of week seven.

Leo asleep in his crib in the little office downstairs.

Last night: I am watching a Herzog film about rental families at an actual theater.

Micheladas.

Modernist, modest, cantilevered, brick and lots of glass on the ground floor.

No mask, no service.

No one at the gastropub on Broome Street.

Not among, not between.

* NOTE: Will reconstruct previous days.

Patrons in the outdoor dining bubbles trying their utmost to maintain a semblance of normality.

Poetry addresses itself to two fundamental limits: death and the barrier of other people's minds, reads the essay.

Saw "An Introduction to Nameless Love" instead.

"Say what you feel not what you ought to say."

Seems ridiculous, but if you insist.

Skip the crowded hugs-free art fair.

Stock up on provisions at the Italian place.

"Swap roles."

The beyondness.

The I Ching recommends "calculated waiting."

The quiet at school the following Monday when we go over.

"The work of the shepherd becomes a kind of loafing."

There is no out.

There, I've said it.

They were all in a pod together.

Tropical mood at the market's taco stand.

Two more dreams unfold one after the other: I am allowed to visit Valeria and she gives me a tour of her duplex somewhere outside the city. She works

from 10–12 pm rain or shine and exactly after twelve hours deletes every-
thing she wrote in the morning.

Two weeks later I'm prepping for an online workshop.

Upbeat signs: "We're open!" "We've missed you!"

Vallejo, lassoer of parenthesis.

Vibrant resonance of life / proportion in space.

Where did this come from?

Why can't I do the same?

Y cada recuerdo es una trampa.

"You must now submit to the fates."

***

OUT OF THE BLUE

"Was your voice always raspy? I mean, in a good way."

Can't answer. Voice is for others to hear.

So I repurpose myself: They took out the singing bowls on Sundays. Strange,
    how the objects wouldn't sound, sometimes, and then, all of a sudden,
    they sung. With a wooden stick, they would surround the rim faster and
    faster until brass sang.

Speak. Scream. Sing.
Speak. Shriek. Spoke.
Song. Sang song.
Singsong.

Sound surrounds. Speeds up, slows
down. Spells stretch. Silence
strikes, softens surfaces.
Surround sound.

She. She. And it, he, and they
and listen.

So you are given a coin. The third side
is song.

Play it back.

ONE FOR YES, TWO FOR NO

I needed the levity so
I said: If you can't find the beat
under the medical gown, the shutdown's become emotional for you.
Then a lump showed up. Minuscule,
heart-adjacent.

Left my right brain. Gotta start somewhere.
First an * ectomy, then a simulation. The rest was a
blast leaving me with a burning
question:
if all humans are mammals.
Did I at me.
One pandemic two pandemics
one is loud another is silent is

                                                             pink

one replicates, the other meta-

a midriff footnote in the form of a rebus: picture of aster
                                        + image of risk

Which looks how
, you might ask.
Does it look like "an emotional complex
in an instant of time." I look up,
accept cookies.

Dreams fill with holes. They recognize me.
I don't. Fatigue the wrong

word but we'll have to make
do. Eleven lead-filled minutes.

Love's reckoning: "As large as I"
double quoted. Nausea as inchoate as the zero-
count jump from millimeters to centimeters.
.4 measuring, sifting...

You do so little.

Ode to the indolent:
"Today I wrote nothing"
to go on quoting.

Languid is the day's word.

NINE POOLS AND A BROKEN GLASS

—After Ed Ruscha

I.

Ash raining on us while horsing
around at the square
pool near the clubhouse
in Cocoyoc. Fields all around
& the scent of burnt sugarcane.
Adults at the tennis court. Premises,
near empty. We didn't understand.
Awareness developing in spurts.
Swam pulls me back,
I come around. No rhyme with *nada*.
Wham.

2.

Funboy
Ibiza bohemia
inflatable kiddie pool.

3.

Like swing
swim is irregular
a verb. "I have swum in that pool before."

We forget to sculpt memories.

4.

"A common reservoir of resources."

5.

Summers in Trumbull.
Swimming in circles
above ground. Chlorine
odor as pungent
as the loop
was deep, relative
to its diameter.
Vinyl. TaB &
Parliament menthol lights.

6.

Drove 58 miles to the world's
largest spring-fed swimming pool, at the Balmorhea State Park.

Recent gator sightings.

FAQ: "How do I get over my fear of jumping in the water?"

7.

Water pooling by the sink shapes a ghoul.

Or: liquid eye & kidney beans.

8.

The Dive Motel

9.

We slip into an infinity pool to cross over to another plane, so otherworldly we risk missing the bus everyone's about to board. This part strikes the dreaming self as nonsense.

10.

A tipsy Argentinian matriarch
lounging poolside takes a tumble;
her wine glass shatters on the hardscape.

The film's tense opening scene.

DREAM CARAVAN DREAM

An exemplary chair marrying wicker and iron. Modern-spirited—its support clean, crisscrossing rods. The seat's materials extracted from and best suited for lounging anywhere in the vast region between the Tropic of Cancer and the Tropic of Capricorn. As if designed for dream recollection, it was sold to me by Déjà Vu and later placed for optimal vantage. I take my seat and gain a view of the wilderness. It all comes back to me then. I teach at an art school that has relocated to Acapulco. I've arrived to run a couple of workshops on repetition. Faculty have transplanted their New England homes to this port city well past its golden era. Only the tents don't clash with the architecture. Under one of them, a group of students in prairie dresses talk ecstatically about L's divination workshop. How do coming events cast their shadows? Sunlight, grasses, breeze. Skin-clinging heat in the form of humidity. Horse-drawn carriages go by. Where are the palm trees? We are not in Appalachia. One of the artists keeps calling out to me by the wrong names: Clara, Lucía, nearly synonymous with lucidity. I'm off to another dream.

My void is called my sister, said the voice I didn't have. Morning thoughts with the consistency of music. A sustained undoneness. Confession distorted, as if in translation. Ions, eons, and other easily confused words. Reduplication or the erotics of indeterminateness, rendered as a series of folds. In a single sentence, such as: "Synapses are plastic." *Me pierdo en el tiempo.* A day's third devoted to shedding dead cells. Analysis, all memory.

Other instances include: "The more a patch of grass is trampled, the clearer the path becomes. A memory of walking is being created." Also wingding, flim-flam, back-to-back. When asked what transpired, she heard herself blurt out: "I am not a revenant!"

Sitting at the edge of the bench, with a partial view of the screen unless I make an effort to see the whole picture. When I do, someone complains that I'm blocking the view. J, sitting in the audience, starts mocking lawmakers who've just passed an outrageous bill in Congress. Expanded cinema. The film is also a book. A young bed-ridden woman seeks her true identity. She finds it at the end, but the knowledge makes all that came before acquire a different meaning. We go back to the beginning. On second read, we realize it's her twin who's discovered her identity. The sisters have been next to each other the whole time. One is clothed and the other one is naked. I turn to the audience and tell them that poetry is law. Explain yourself, someone demands. We owe our feelings, don't we, I ask. The audience begins to disperse; a tourist who's announced he's lodging at the Seasons Hotel watches me put my boots back on after I wipe my feet clean. The floor is full of dirt. The last scene is a close up of feet. One twin is the right foot, the other one is left.

A healing ritual is being performed on me at a fulfilment center. I'm lying down on a massage table as the proprietor and her lookalike daughter slide their hands a few inches away from my aura methodically from head to toe. Waves of pleasure ripple through my entire body. When they stop, I start readying myself to leave but the younger one stops me, "Wait, we're not done yet!" She takes my right breast in her hands and, from my own flesh, begins sculpting the head of "the baby I never had." It has a glimmer in its eyes, puckers its lips as if grinning, and makes gurgling sounds that speak to me. It's warm and beautiful and I show it to B, who's materialized in the room all of a sudden. I take us elsewhere as soon as I remember all those people waiting in line outside.

Two editions of a nonexistent book. A probable book in which New York School poets discuss the composition of their works. I'm participating in the launch and have travelled with a group to a city reminiscent of Tokyo. We're trying to find the venue and enter the wrong building. The more we get lost, the less I remember what I'd planned to say. A asks me to go fetch her copy of the book, which she forgot at the hotel. I get even more lost but manage to locate it. Her copy includes a facsimile of her journals. I can't find the pages I'd earmarked in my own copy of the second edition. I walk into the auditorium a half hour late carrying a giant, filthy vat in each hand which I proceed to hide behind velvet curtains.

The poets are seated at a picnic table onstage and there's a Ouija board on the table. M is there. The other A is there too. She tells me to sit on the bench across from her. I would prefer not to: if I want to face the audience, I'd have to turn my back to the other panelists. Also there, D and G with her new boyfriend, though it's not G, it's B. I'm still sore that she lied to me. I'm trapped onstage. I am relieved when the moderator begins querying us about our own creative processes. There are two planes: one exterior and one interior. The first requires that your antennas are out, that you allow yourself to be guided by whatever is happening outside. The interior one, on the other hand, is like a square by Josef Albers inside another square that is the interior of an exterior interior. I lose my train of thought but the moderator doesn't notice. Her fingers are gliding on the Ouija board.

Identical tear marks in the same spot of the sky on consecutive days. Rows of dolphins propel themselves in the sound. I am with a group of animated, highly sociable mammals. To go from one part of town to another, both equidistant from the shore, we must walk on the beach. No one but me sees them dipping in and out of the water, fins and arched backs glistening off in the distance. Mirrored processions, unalike speeds.

A pit bull lunges toward us on the trail. Its equally thick-set owner makes half-assed attempts at calling it back. I see flashes of torn skin and oozing blood in my mind's eye. B uses the oversize umbrella he's been lugging as a shield to shoo away the dog. It stops. Its owner struggles to catch up to it. Once he does, he fastens a leash onto its collar. Adrenaline rushes as it starts to pour. We quicken our step. A few minutes later, we hear shouts from behind once more. I'm shaking. There's the dog again, though this time it approaches us with an amicable gait. A kid catches up to him, fastens a leash onto its collar. A different dog. A retriever or lab, also honey-colored.

"Probably a Maga guy. Fucking asshole. Can't wait to see the car he's driving."

We pass a tree on whose bare branch someone put a lost glove, giving the finger.

"That's the spirit."

At the parking lot, there's a Vibe just like ours next to our car. The bald eagle decorating the hood is painted flamingo pink. From the mirror hang beads ending in a heart charm. The dashboard is covered in ornaments: fuzz balls in bright colors and a monarch butterfly. A stack of flags rests on the backseat.

I repeat the poem in Spanish a number of times so I can transcribe it upon waking. It's so simple I can't possibly forget it. Later a search takes me to the sole extant recording of Alejandra Pizarnik's voice. She reads a poem by Arturo Carrera whose title translates to "Written with a Nyctograph." *El escriba ha desaparecido.*

The phrase "future historian of feelings" in another notebook. *El poema se abre.* Remembering's sediments. *Esa es tu fuerza.* Only a translator might be able to decode them according to the cathartic method. I am given a book of hers wrapped in kraft paper. No trace of the poem, just a password in gift form.

We are staying at a hotel reminiscent of the one in *Last Year in Marienbad* with our friends. He leaves me a coded message suggesting that we meet on our own. I am excited by his proposition and show up at the room at the end of a long corridor at the arranged time. His wife opens the door and instantly realizes what's happening. On my way there, I was planning to call things off. Not worth it, I was going to say. We'd risk ruining our friendship forever. But it's too late. His wife thinks the worse has already happened. I assure her there's nothing going on between us, but everything I say makes matters worse. She's crying. I'm crying. He arrives, mortified. B arrives. His wife delivers the news to him, delivers the news to B. Misunderstandings and projections are already causing irreparable damage. It's a nightmare. A telenovela. No comedy of errors. I am overcome by guilt and despair. I should've known better. Something about his paintings had always suggested this kind of imbroglio to me. He gets on his knees and apologizes to the three of us.

We decide to take the poodle for a walk around the hotel and talk things out. As we're doing that, the grounds rotate 180 degrees. I dream I wake up horrified at my behavior, fall asleep again, and begin the same dream again, but with an entirely different orientation. It dawns on me: this is a novel's perfect structure.

COLLECTION BEISTEGUI, SALLE 714

Here, hardly any indices of modernity's disquiets.
Portraits of noble patrons and intimate relations,
often indistinguishable, line the walls, alongside
an anonymous Madonna and child and a sketch
for a painting of Napoleon. Also portrayed: an ill
and cultivated countess from Bilbao; Dido in the act
of taking her own life with a sword, her lover's;
and artists whose gazes hint at a will to manifest
the otherwise unseen. The collector stands out
among the personages of myth and rarefied society,
for, in his picture, doubles of a couple of oils
in the gallery adorn also the wall behind him:
the Rococo portrait of an artist's wife and two thirds
of one Mme Panckoucke. Zuloaga, its author,
mutes the color of the canvases inside the canvas,
bestowing added luster on his subject Carlos
de Beistegui, and on his bald head especially.
This is no cartoon and the sitter shouldn't be taken
for Charlie, his more colorful nephew, collector too,
interior decorator, and lover of copies and trompe l'oeil.
Unconcerned with expressing his inner life's
rumblings, M. Beistegui appears eager to resume
deciphering insignia on the rare coins
on the table beside him. The shine in his eyes
betrays his sublimated extraction, the family's fortune
from silver-mining in Mexico—a place they fled
upon Maximilian's execution which he must've visited
as rarely as I visit the Louvre. I want to return
to the painting of the young Countess del Carpio,

author of a sentimental comedy, dead from consumption
months after being rendered, the flight of her shadow
compared by an elegist to "a wandering cloud's."
The draw, how Goya captured her unbecoming
condition, her resolve expiring under the volume
of the outlandish pink bow gracing her thinning hair.
Her not saying, "Héme aquí, inmortalizada."

WEEPING WILLOW: A LYRIC

Willow wept.
I am in the past waiting,
waiting for the future
to bring me your ears which are your eyes
your Is your ayes
Weeping, weeping willow.
Willow wept.

Raindrops fuller than tears
sliding down the fresh green curtain of its boughs.
Pools cleansing the dark mystery of hatred—
its irreparable harms.

Weeping, weeping willow.
I am in the past waiting,
waiting for the future
to bring me your ears so you can hear
the small glory of being
able to mourn,
of being able to carry, attune.

BOGOTÁ NOTEBOOK

Mentiría si escribiera que volví intacta.

No one returns unmoved from Bogotá.
Movement is the subject we've been summoned
to activate collectively. The kinesics
and kinetics of bodies shifting with each other.
No one's hung up on difference. The landscape's
craggy edges soften when the greenery of the Andes
vibrates in the surrounding hills, in the bodies
performing at the night market for medicinal plants.

"La noche es el manicomio de las plantas."

Night is plant life's madhouse.

Pasaron cosas, pasaron como pasan cuando están pasando,
pasan, estaban sucediendo, pero no habrá más sucesión,
porque a Colón y la Reina Isabel ya nadie los quiere
ver, y si los llegaras a ver, imagínate que no los viste
y no les tomes fotos. No photos. No posts.

Things kept happening, as when they are coming to pass,
they pass, meaning, in Spanish, that they're taking place,
and overtaking is no longer commended, so patrimony
and memory management officials preemptively removed
Columbus and Queen Isabella of Castile from their pedestals
flanking the avenue which never led to El Dorado.

Time is golden. History is not.

Moved to a secret location before the Misak peoples toppled them,
beheading them perhaps; before they would meet the same fate
as the statue of Quesada, founder of the city, toppled,
for whom the Muisca peoples performed mortuary rituals,
since when felled, he fell on his face, signaling his regret.
Their rituals cleansed him and, through forgiveness,
rid the city of colonial toxicity.

Womb city purified.

The relocated statues and artists in the live arts
converge in a reclaimed train station in Bogotá,
statues half-hidden behind a skimpy tarp,
insufficient given their monumentality.

*

Upon arrival, we sit around a tree in an enclosed garden.

We thank the genii locorum for receiving us, placing shells around a magnifi-
cent trunk.

The remnants of ritual, fragments of stories of those sitting nearest me.

Saeed born to an Iranian father and a Mexican mother in Aguascalientes and
Luis who I never see dance, who went to the same grade school as the
magical realist in Zipaquirá and is a student of unknowing.

My power circle peeps. My provisional coterie. *Mis chismosas.*

We lock gazes and choreograph our words.

Yo te veo. Tú me ves.

I see you. You see me.

    Yo te veo. Tú me ves.

We walk in circles, careful not to step on slugs and other organic matter, until we find a space to ground us.

I sit on the piece of an old train track that reminds me of the rods in my scoliotic spine.

It's been so long since I saw my distorted body reflected in somebody else's pupils.

Cuerpo etc. Expanded movement practices.

Cuerpa cuerpo cuerpe etc. A new neo-Baroque.

We receive healing instruction.

Those of us with vulvas practice breathwork and activate our organ's energetic channels away from the statue's frozen gazes.

Ser una en varias. To be one in many.

> We do a vulva
> practice—oh, dear organ. I had
> forgotten you so.

>   Práctica vulva
>   órgano esencial y el
>   menos cuidado.

Breathing we're anchored,
we channel the syllables,
crystals of process.

Expand me my flesh my contours Plexiglas high-filtration ultra-fine fibers.

Listen to an alien language and touch someone else as if touch didn't touch.

Gather between what's intentionally left unfinished and the unintentionally unfinished.

Return to the enclosed garden and hear the correspondences.

Witness the traces of those forced to work their love in secret at the station, hear the channeling of their voices.

Dance the vestiges of the warrior dance until in a trance you return to the enclosed garden once again.

To learn to let go, find a spot to dig a hole to bury a decomposing body collectively formed with spit hair rotting fruit horrid and gorgeously lacking in facial features.

An exquisitely putrid lump of organic matter swathed in a wet, sullied shroud getting heavier and moister on a plastic tarp.

Buried so we can find the first person.

Salt from Zipaquirá will not cleanse the stench. Mint leaves half-trick the senses.

Bury the bright, pungent rot under a glorious Chinese lantern shrub.

A perfect site to leave there, half-buried, our offering.

***

Notes

"Feliza": *¡Hágase la loca!* is a fragment of a quote by Colombian artist Feliza Bursztyn (1933–1982). The full quote, "En un país de machistas, hágase la loca" (In a country of machos, pretend you're a madwoman) appears as the title of a 1979 interview in the magazine *Carrusel*.

"Parable": The poem is for Caroline Bergvall. The second section takes language from different translations of the phrase "confuses paroles" in Baudelaire's "Correspondances." The first two lines read: "La Nature est un temple où de vivants piliers / Laissent parfois sortir de confuses paroles…" "Confused words" is from William Aggeler's translation (1954); "subdued words," from Cyril Scott's (1909); "vague words," from Roy Campbell's (1952): "a soft language, half strange, half understood" appears in George Dillon's (1936); "darkling whispers," in Lewis Piaget Shanks's (1931); and "perplexing messages," in Richard Howard's (1982). "Shimmers of verbal nuance" appears in an experimental version by Rachel Blau DuPlessis (2015).

"Saucer Magnolia": This poem sources language from Michael A. Dirr's *Manual of Woody Landscape Plants: Their Identification, Ornamental Characteristics, Culture, Propagation and Uses* (Champaign, IL: Stipes Publishing, 1988) and *Encyclopedia of Trees and Shrubs* (Portland, OR: Timber Press, 2011). Information about the first specimens available at the Linnaean Botanic Garden in Flushing Queens appears in "The saucer magnolia" by David H. in "Growing History: The Philadelphia Historic Plants Consortium," posted on Oct. 14, 2012. The quote from Solange-Boudin's diaries is from "A modest tribute to Étienne Soulange-Bodin at this late date," by Carl R. Amason, *AMS Newsletter*, Spring-Summer 1976. The botanist's praise of culture is taken from his *Notice sur une novelle espéce de Magnolia* (Decourchant et Gallay, 1826).

"London Plane Tree": Besides weaving in overheard language, the poem sources language found in Michael Dirr's *Manual of Woody Landscape Plants*.

"The Lombard Effect": "The vociferous song is of course in complete opposition to their observability." James Duncan, "Nightingale–Bird Song," https://sussexwildlifetrust.org.uk/news/nightingale-bird-song. Accessed Sept. 21, 2023.

"Sunstead": "hell itself breathes out contagion to this world" *Hamlet*, 3.2.388-390

"Prompt": Javier Marías, *Bad Nature, or with Elvis in Mexico,* trans. Esther Allen (New York: New Directions, 2010).

"Priority Was Handwritten": The poem is for Ian Anderson.

"Triple Turn and Skip": A literal translation of the lines in the poem is: "it is March March it is / March is march / is to love each other is Mars god of war / to go to Mars is to love you and to march / the march of days and the battle / yes the battle goes on yes there are circles / that remain open and circles that are closed / circles that are closed circles that remain open / there are circles circles and circles semicircles or incomplete circumferences / there are circles that are circles that are ripples in the shallowest part / of liquid surfaces that are waves and circles that are sound waves / circles that are sounds that have left or that are nests / there are circles that are nests and circles that have left / continuing themselves in a circle in a spiral / circles never close / the circles." The word-play in the poem, in which, for instance, breaking up the word *sonidos* (sounds) yields the phrases, *son nidos* (are nests) or *son idos* (have left), could be recreated in English using entirely different words.

"Nine Pools and a Broken Glass": The poem takes its title and form from Ed Ruscha's artist's book *Nine Swimming Pools and a Broken Glass* (Los Angeles: Heavy Industry, 1968).

"Weeping Willow": The Spanish in the poem is the chorus in "Cielito Lindo," a Mexican folksong composed by Quirino Mendoza y Cortés in 1882.

"Bogotá Notebook": "La noche es el manicomio de las plantas." Raúl Zurita, *Purgatorio*, trans. Anna Deeny (Berkeley: University of California Press, 2009).

Acknowledgments

Grateful acknowledgment to the editors of the journals and publications in which earlier versions of the following poems appeared.

128 Lit: "Priority Was Handwritten"; *A Perfect Vacuum:* "Closet Drama" ("Last March"), "Last February," and "Last January"; *The Baffler*: "Fit to Print"; *BOMB*: "Feliza" and "The Lombard Effect"; *Broadcast* by Pioneer Works: "Dream Caravan Dream"; *The Brooklyn Rail*: "One for Yes, Two for No" and "Phantom"; *Changes Review*: "Parable" and "Obverse"; *Departures*: "Distance Calculator"; *Harper's*: "Not Against the Rules"; *Magazine – MoMA*: "Nine Pools and A Broken Glass"; *Midst*: "December"; *New York Review of Books*: "That August"; *Paperbag*: "After This, Begin Jumps," "Did you accidentally summon me?," "Word Scrambler," "Sunstead," and "Bogotá Notebook"; *The Paris Review*: "Flip Side"; *PLACE Revue d'art / Art magazine*: "Feliza," "Saucer Magnolia," and "A Year and a Day"; *Poem-A-Day* (selected by Claudia Rankine): "Theorem of Sorts"; *Poetry Magazine*: "Last March," "Return to Psychogeography" ("Last May") and "That March"; *Viseu.us*: "Copse," "London Plane Tree" (both in collaboration with Hans Tammen)

"Parable" appears in *Caroline Bergvall's Medievalist Poetics: Migratory Texts and Transhistorical Methods*, edited by Caroline Bergvall and Joshua Davis (ARC Humanities Press, 2023).

"Out of the Blue" appears in the artist's book *Playlist* by Suzanne McClelland (Space Sisters Press, 2019).

"Ahí viene el lobo" appears in *Creature Needs: Writers Respond to the Science of Animal Conservation*, edited by Christopher Kondrich, Susan Tacent, and Lucy Spelman (University of Minnesota, 2024).

"Collection Beistegui, Salle 714" appears in the anthology *Poems of the Louvre* (NYRB, 2024) and, in French translation, in *Poésie du Louvre* (Seghers, 2024).

"Parable," "Saucer Magnolia," "After This, Begin Jumps," "London Plane Tree," "The Lombard Effect," "Sycamore: A Lyric," "Then Again," and "Weeping Willow: A Lyric" are part of a collaboration with sound artist Hans Tammen titled *Arboretum* developed while participating in the Harvestworks Artist in Residence Program in 2023. Our eight-channel sound installation was included in the exhibition "New Waves in Art and Tech" at

Harvestworks Art and Technology Building on Governors Island from May 17–Aug. 18, 2024. Special thanks to Carol Parkinson and Kevin Ramsay at Harvestworks.

I am grateful to my students at Brooklyn College and Julie Agoos, Eurídice Arratia, Jane Ayers, Alex Balgiu, Mary Jo Bang, Charles Bernstein, Anselm Berrigan, Timothy Donnelly, Moriah Evans, David Everitt Howe, Farnoosh Fathi, Diego Gerard, Alan Gilbert, Peter Gizzi, Lucía Hinojosa Gaxiola, Richard Kraft, Annette Leddy, Ben Lerner, Tan Lin, Suzanne McClelland, Jenny Monick, Urayoán Noel, Lisa Pearson, Claudia Rankine, Kim Rosenfield, Eleni Sikelianos, Steel Stillman, Srikanth Reddy, Hans Tammen, Laureana Toledo, Ellen Tremper, Matvei Yankelevich, and Lynn Xu for supporting my work in various ways.

A Bruce Pearson y Shadow y a la familia, todo mi amor y gracias siempre.

Much gratitude to Wenzel Bilger, then director of the Goethe-Institut Bogotá, and all those who hosted and organized the events for the Encuentro de Prácticas Expandidas del Movimiento en Suramérica *Cuerpo etc.* in the fall of 2021. This was a gathering in which Latin American artists in the field of expanded movement practices led workshops and collective actions.

Thanks to the Lucas Artists Residency Program at the Montalvo Arts Center and to Derek Beaulieu and the Banff Centre for Arts and Creativity for giving me the space and time to begin and finish this book.

Without the vision and tireless efforts of Stephen Motika, Kit Schluter, Lindsey Bolt, Emily Bark Brown, Lina Bergamini, and Dante Silva at Nightboat Books these pages wouldn't be here.

A grant from Creative Capital in 2022 and the C.D. Wright Award for Poetry from the Foundation for Contemporary Arts made this work possible. Much appreciation to everyone who helps these foundations continue to support artists.

MÓNICA DE LA TORRE was born and raised in Mexico City and is based in New York City. Previous poetry books include *Repetition Nineteen* (2020), which centers on experimental translation; *The Happy End/All Welcome* (2017)—a riff on a riff on Kafka's *Amerika*—and *Public Domain* (2009). She is co-editor of the international anthology *Women in Concrete Poetry, 1959–1979* (2020) and the recipient of the 2022 Foundation for Contemporary Arts C.D. Wright Award for Poetry and a 2022 Creative Capital grant. She teaches at Brooklyn College.

NIGHTBOAT BOOKS

Nightboat Books, a nonprofit organization, seeks to develop audiences for writers whose work resists convention and transcends boundaries. We publish books rich with poignancy, intelligence, and risk. Please visit nightboat.org to learn about our titles and how you can support our future publications.

The following individuals have supported the publication of this book. We thank them for their generosity and commitment to the mission of Nightboat Books:

Kazim Ali, Anonymous (8), Mary Armantrout, Jean C. Ballantyne, Thomas Ballantyne, Bill Bruns, John Cappetta, V. Shannon Clyne, Ulla Dydo Charitable Fund, Photios Giovanis, Amanda Greenberger, Vandana Khanna, Isaac Klausner, Shari Leinwand, Anne Marie Macari, Elizabeth Madans , Martha Melvoin, Caren Motika, Elizabeth Motika, The Leslie Scalapino - O Books Fund, Robin Shanus, Thomas Shardlow, Rebecca Shea, Ira Silverberg, Benjamin Taylor, David Wall, Jerrie Whitfield & Richard Motika, Arden Wohl, Issam Zineh

This book is made possible, in part, by grants from the New York City Department of Cultural Affairs in partnership with the City Council, the National Endowment for the Arts, and the New York State Council on the Arts Literature Program.